"WIZZIE"
THE LIFE AND ADVENTURES OF
NORMAN WISDOM

Written by

Kevin Powis

Address: Via www.KevinPowis.com
Phone Number: UK : 0800 612 8996

OVER BLACK.

SUPERIMPOSE:

"Such is life and life is such
and after all it isn't much.
First a cradle. Then a hearse.
It might have been better,
but could have been worse."

Sir Norman Wisdom
1915-2010

                                                    FADE IN:

EXT. LONDON STREET - BAFTA AWARDS 1954 (BLACK AND WHITE)

SUPERIMPOSE: BAFTA Awards, London 1954.

Crowds jostle and photographers clamber for position.
Familiar looking actors of the period wave and walk on by.
As, in the style of a Pathe' Newsreel a stiff upper lipped
NARRATOR speaks to the nation.

                    NARRATOR
          There goes Jack Hawkins. He's
          leaving the ladies swooning.
          Nominated for a second year. This
          time for his outstanding
          performance in "The Cruel Sea".

A limousine pulls up at the grand event. The cameras flash.
NORMAN[37], his mother MAUD and agent BILLY MARSH climb out
to be welcomed by adoring fans and camera flashes.

                    NARRATOR (CONT'D)
          And who's this? None other than
          comedian Norman Wisdom. The new kid
          on the block. Norman will be hoping
          to pick up the award for "Most
          Promising Newcomer" following the
          sell out success of his new film,
          "Trouble in Store."

Norman waves. The door of the limousine slams shut.

                                                    CUT TO:

EXT. LONDON STREET - CONTINUOUS (COLOUR)

Maud in shock.

                        MAUD
          Oh Norman! What have you done?

                        NORMAN[37]
          Come on Mom, enjoy it. Keep up and
          keep smiling.

Norman trips over his own foot and the crowd lap it up. The
bulbs continue to flash and the trio smile and wave in every
direction making their way along the red carpet.

                        BILLY MARSH
          Who would have thought it Norm.
          You're an overnight success.

The bulb flashes intensify.

                        NORMAN[37]
          Overnight? You.. Anyway, you know
          me Billy. I've always been a lucky
          little devil.

Norman gives Billy a friendly nudge. The flashes intensify
further and Norman holds out a palm shield his eyes as he
looks back to locate Maud.

Flash, Flash..

                        NORMAN[37] (CONT'D)
          Mom?

A blinding white flash fills the screen.

                                        CUT TO WHITE:

                                        FADE IN:

FLASHBACK - EXT. LONDON STREET - 1923 - DAY

SUPERIMPOSE: London 1923.

Scruffy urchin like children, including NORMAN[8] and his
elder brother YOUNG FRED (10), are play fighting with other
boys in the drab street. Looking out of place, parked in the
road outside one of the houses, is a very smart and expensive
limousine. Norman[8] catches sight of a young woman, hurrying
out of the front door of the same house, carrying a suitcase.
Norman[8] stops in his tracks and watches with a puzzled look
as she scurries away quickly down the street.

                        NORMAN[8]
          Mom?

She doesn't look. Young Fred and Norman watch her disappear
and then dart towards the house.

                                        CUT TO:

INT. FAMILY HOUSE - 1923

The room is dark. Hanging up on a hook, is a chauffeur's
uniform. NORMAN'S DAD sits biting at the thumb of a clenched
fist and staring at the floor.

                    YOUNG FRED (O.S.)
          Dad!

Norman[8] and Young Fred burst into the room.

                    YOUNG FRED (CONT'D)
          Where's Mom gone?

                    NORMAN[8]
          Dad?

                    NORMAN'S DAD
             (crying)
          She's left me. You better get used
          to it because this time she ain't
          coming back.

Fred starts to cry. Norman doesn't. He stands forward.

                    NORMAN[8]
          Don't say that.

                    NORMAN'S DAD
          Get out my sight.

Norman's Dad gets up to walk away.

                    NORMAN[8]
          No--

Before he can finish his sentence, Norman's Dad hits out at
Norman[8] and sends him sprawling. Young Fred rushes to help
him up. Norman's Dad glares at them both and walks out. A
DOOR SLAMS off screen. Young Fred and Norman[8] are left
alone and huddle together on the floor.

                                        CUT TO:

EXT. LONDON STREET - 1923 - SOME DAYS LATER - DAY

Norman[8] and Young Fred are watching nearby market traders
and are most interested in a fruit store. They fane interest
as a MARKET TRADER calls out with cockney market banter.

                    MARKET TRADER
          Come on now ladies, buy one get one
          free. And no Misses, you can't just
          have the free one!

The boys slide closer and the trader plays to the attention
of his young audience. Every time the trader turns the boys
are taking apples and shoving them up their jumpers and in
their trouser pockets.

                    MARKET TRADER (CONT'D)
          Ladies, come and get your spuds
          here. Cheap as chips!

A woman takes the offer. And Norman bags another apple..

                    MARKET TRADER (CONT'D)
          There you go love. You know I only
          have eyes for you!

..The trader sees him.

                    MARKET TRADER (CONT'D)
          Oi! You bloody thieves..

He makes a grab for Norman[8] but he's too quick.

                                        CUT TO:

EXT. LONDON STREET - CONTINUOUS

Norman[8] and Young Fred comes bounding round the corner
belly laughing uncontrollably after their getaway. And
Norman[8] runs straight into the path of a WOMAN ON A BIKE.

He goes tumbling over, apples everywhere. The Woman saves
herself but she's distraught. She put's down the bike and
rushes to Norman[8].

                    WOMAN ON A BIKE
          Oh, I'm so sorry are you hurt?

                    NORMAN[8]
          I.. I don't know. How can I tell?

                    WOMAN ON A BIKE
          Well can you move everything?

                    NORMAN[8]
          Yes. Course I can. Look.

Norman[8] jiggles.

                    WOMAN ON A BIKE
          Oh thank goodness.

She helps him up.

                    WOMAN ON A BIKE (CONT'D)
          So, do you have any pain anywhere?

Norman[8] pats himself down. Then stops around his trousers.

                    NORMAN[8]
          Me sixpence.

                    WOMAN ON A BIKE
          Oh dear. You're hurt? Down there?

                    NORMAN[8]
          No, Miss. I've lost me sixpence. I
          had sixpence my Dad gave me. He'll
          go mad.

                    WOMAN ON A BIKE
          Oh, wait.

She looks in a purse and pulls out a shilling.

                    WOMAN ON A BIKE (CONT'D)
          Here you go. I'm just pleased
          you're not hurt.

                    NORMAN[8]
          Oh, thank you miss.

The woman mounts her bike, RINGS the BELL and rides off.

                    YOUNG FRED
          Norm? Dad would never give anyone a
          sixpence especially you.

                    NORMAN[8]
              (resigned)
          I know. Help me pick up me apples?

                              DISSOLVE TO:

EXT. LONDON STREET - 1923 - HIDDEN AWAY - DAY

Short silence as Norman[8] and Young Fred sit eating their
apples, before..

                    NORMAN[8]
          When's Dad coming back?

                    YOUNG FRED
          You know as much as me Norm. He has
          to drive that posh bloke whereever
          he wants to go.

More chewing.

                    NORMAN[8]
          When's Mom coming back?

                    YOUNG FRED
               (sigh)
          She's ain't Norm. Dad's told ya.

                    NORMAN[8]
          Why can't we live with her instead
          of Dad.

                    YOUNG FRED
          She's got her own posh bloke now.
          They don't want you hanging around,
          making the place untidy.

There's a small silence.

                    YOUNG FRED (CONT'D)
          He said he's gonna' board us out.

                    NORMAN[8]
          Why? What's happened to his belt?

                    YOUNG FRED
          No Norm. He'll let us stay with
          someone else. They'll feed us too.
          No more scraps.

                    NORMAN[8]
          Good, cos these apples are giving
          me the belly ache.

                    YOUNG FRED
               (laughs)
          You're funny Norm! Belly ache..

                                        CUT TO:

INT. SCHOOL ROOM - 1923

1920's school room. Rows of desks with scruffy children
occupying them. Towering over a seated Norman[8] stands a
very large and menacing teacher MR.HARRIS. He is holding a
wooden ruler and slapping it in to his palm.

                    MR.HARRIS
          Belly ache! Belly ache!
          What do you mean, belly ache?

                    NORMAN[8]
          It's the apples.

                    MR.HARRIS
               (menacing)
          Where are you getting apples from
          Wisdom? You're a feral urchin.

                    NORMAN[8]
          Thank you Sir.

The class laughs but Norman[8] gets the ruler slammed on his
hand. He doesn't show the pain. The class winces in unison.

                    MR.HARRIS
          Still got belly ache Wisdom?

                    NORMAN[8]
          Yes Sir and now me hand hurts too.

The class laugh again. Mr. Harris grabs Norman's sleeve and
flexes for another shot. He decides enough.

                    MR.HARRIS
          Get to the toilet and hurry back.

Some of the class snigger as Norman leaves the class.

                    MR.HARRIS (CONT'D)
          Silent reading!

                                        CUT TO:

INT. SCHOOL ROOM - CORRIDOR - 1923

Norman[8] closes the door now holds his hand and runs.

                                        CUT TO:

EXT. FAMILY HOUSE - 1923 - DAY

Norman[8] comes to a rapid stop when he sees the posh car
parked in front and realises his Dad is back home. He turns
and runs in the opposite direction.

                                        DISSOLVE TO:

EXT. LONDON STREET - 1920'S - DAY - LATER

Norman[8] is sitting on the wall waiting for Fred to come
home from school. He finally sees him turn the corner.

                        YOUNG FRED
                Norm! Where you been?

Norman[8] drops from the wall and goes to him. Fred, grabs
hold of Norman[8]'s bruised hand to get a closer look.

                        NORMAN[8]
                Dad's home.

Fred drops Norman[8]'s hand.

                        YOUNG FRED
                Is he? Well he's gonna go mad when
                he see's that. Best say you've been
                in a fight. I'll back you up.

The two walk home. Norman[8] pretends to be fighting,
punching the air.

                        NORMAN[8]
                Yes, I was in a fight. I could be a
                boxer when I grow up.

                        YOUNG FRED
                    (laughs)
                You might get a job boxing apples
                that's all.

They laugh. Norman[8] sparring the air as they walk away.

                                        CUT TO:

INT. HOUSE - 1923 - LATER

Norman[8] and Young Fred walk into the house. They stop dead
when they see the teacher Mr.Harris is there drinking tea
with their father.

The mood is dark. Mr.Harris puts down his cup, excuses himself politely with a slight nod to their father, picks up his hat, calmly places it on his head and leaves giving Norman[8] a hard threatening glare. Norman's Dad stands and slowly undoes his belt buckle and pulls his thick leather belt from his trousers.

                    YOUNG FRED
          Norm!

Norman[8] makes a dive for the door but it's no use.

                                        CUT TO WHITE:

                                        FADE IN:

EXT. LONDON HOTEL - 1928 - DAY

SUPERIMPOSE: London, 1928.

An older NORMAN[13] checks the address of a London hotel against a scrap of paper from his pocket.

                                        CUT TO:

INT. LONDON HOTEL - 1928 - MINUTES LATER

A young boy, JOE, who speaks with a very strong Welsh accent is waking through the hotel with Norman[13]. A young girl, SALLY, catches Norman[13]'s eye as she walks past.

                    SALLY
          Morning.

                    JOE
          Morning.

                    NORMAN[13]
               (shy)
          Morning.

                    JOE
               (quiet)
          That's Sally. Just one of the many
          benefits of working here. This is a
          easy number Norman. Keep your head
          down and you'll be all right.

Norman[13] tries a fake Welsh accent.

                    NORMAN[13]
          All right Boyoh.

Joe puts his hand on Norman[13]'s shoulder as they walk away
both smiling.

                    JOE
          Oh, we're gonna get on fine. I like
          a joke.

                    NORMAN[13]
          Me too. Nothing I like better.

                                        CUT TO:

INT. LONDON HOTEL - 1928 - KITCHEN

They arrive in the kitchen. Kitchen staff, working, food
everywhere. Norman[13] takes it all in. Joe gestures to the
mountains of food in front of them.

                    JOE
          You won't go hungry working here.
          You can have anything you want.
          Just help yourself.

Norman[13] picks up a cake from a fancy cake stand.

                    JOE (CONT'D)
               (quiet)
          Tuck in. You lucky little devil!

Norman[13] brings the cake to his mouth. Before.. a mighty
SMACK comes from behind sending the cake into his face.
Norman[13] turns, covered in cream, to see MR.GRACE. Very
tall and formal in full black suit.

                    MR.GRACE
          And what exactly are you're doing?

                    NORMAN[13]
          I.. I--

                    JOE
          He's new Mr. Grace. The job centre
          sent him. I'll soon sort him out.

                    MR.GRACE
          Get out of my kitchen.

                    JOE
          He's going Mr.Grace.

Joe grabs Norman and leads him away.

                    NORMAN[13]
          You said I could have anything..

                    JOE
          I forgot to say you can only do
          that when no one is looking.
          Oh, we're going to have such fun.
          Come on.

                                        DISSOLVE TO:

MONTAGE - LONDON HOTEL - VARIOUS

- Norman carrying trays to and from the rooms.

- Cleaning shoes and carrying case.

- Running errands, upstairs, down stairs.

- Rising early morning

- Dropping into his bunk late at night.

END OF MONTAGE

                                        DISSOLVE TO:

INT. LONDON HOTEL - 1928 - SCULLERY - EVENING

SUPER: "Six Months Later."

It's late and Joe and Norman[13] cleaning a pile of shoes.

                    JOE
          Do you miss home Norm?

                    NORMAN[13]
          No, not a bit. You?

                    JOE
          Oh Yes. Wales is fantastic see. You
          should come back with me. We could
          clean up there.

                    NORMAN[13]
          We're cleaning up here ain't we?
          You ain't leaving are you?

                    JOE
          I know you'll miss me but I am
          indeed, any day now.

                    NORMAN[13]
How come?

                    JOE
Things are picking up back home and
the pits are hiring again.

                    NORMAN[13]
Really?

                    JOE
Oh yes. And better money than we'll
ever see here. And the girls are
better in Wales too. Not stuck up
like they are round here.

                    NORMAN[13]
Sally's nice.

                    JOE
Oh, "Sally's Nice". You've got no
chance mate.

                    NORMAN[13]
She always says hello.

                    JOE
She probably feels sorry for you
and let's be honest no one can
blame her for that. But wake up
Boyoh. You're a Page Boy. You're
like something on the bottom of one
of these shoes round here.

Norman[13] can only agree.

                    JOE (CONT'D)
Look, why don't you come with me?

                    NORMAN[13]
I couldn't do that.

                    JOE
Have you ever been to Wales?

                    NORMAN[13]
No..but..

                    JOE
Well then. That's even more reason
you should come. You're a man of
the world ain't you? Or do you want
to be cleaning dirt off other
people's shoes all your life?

                         NORMAN[13]
          Yes, I mean no. Oh! How would we
          even get there?

                         JOE
          We walk. How else?

                         NORMAN[13]
          Walk?

                         JOE
          Why not? We can sneak as much food
          as we need from the kitchen. It'll
          be an adventure!

Joe is too busy looking at Norman[13] to notice that he has
picked up a light coloured shoe and is polishing it with
black polish.

                         JOE (CONT'D)
          What do you think?

Norman notices what is happening.

                         JOE (CONT'D)
          You can board with my folks. I'll
          write home and by the time we get
          there they'll have jobs waiting for
          both of us.

                         NORMAN[13]
          You know what I think?

                         JOE
          Go on..

                         NORMAN[13]
          You're blacking brown leather.

Joe throws down the shoe in disgust.

                         JOE
          Oh, never mind that! What about it?

                         NORMAN[13]
          I wouldn't want to be you when
          Mr.Grace finds out you're planning
          to leave.

                         JOE
          He don't scare me. I'll tell him to
          his face what I really think and
          quit on the spot. He can like it or
          lump it.

                        JOE (CONT'D)
When I leave here, I'll walk out
with my head held high. Think about
coming with me Norm. I know you
want to. It would be great.

Norman[13] is left pondering.

                        JOE (CONT'D)
Me or Sally? Whose it gonna be?

Norman[13] throws a show at Joe.

                                        CUT TO:

INT. LONDON HOTEL - 1928 LOBBY - NEXT DAY

Norman[13] wants to speak to Sally and is pretending to be
working as he gets nearer and nearer to her. Sally is busy,
she doesn't notice him. Eventually from behind a vase..

                        NORMAN[13]
Hello Sally.

She jumps.

                        SALLY
Oh! Hello Norman.

                        NORMAN[13]
Sally?

                        SALLY
Yes Norman.

                        NORMAN[13]
I was wondering?

                        SALLY
Wondering what?

                        NORMAN[13]
Well they're showing a new film at
the Plaza tonight.

                        SALLY
Are they? That's nice.

                        NORMAN[13]
Well I was wondering?

                        SALLY
Do a lot of wondering do you?

                         NORMAN[13]
              Eh? Oh yes. I'm always wondering
              here and wondering there.

                         SALLY
              Funny too!

                         NORMAN[13]
              Oh do you think so?

                         SALLY
              Not really Norman.

Shot down.

                         NORMAN[13]
              Oh, well anyway, I was wondering--

                         SALLY
              If I'd go with you.

                         NORMAN[13]
              Oh? Well would ya? My treat.

Sally stops what she's doing to deliver terms.

                         SALLY
              I'm not a cheap date Norman so if
              you think you can really afford to
              take me out I finish at six.

He wasn't expecting that.

                         NORMAN[13]
              A date? Oh! Right! Brilliant.

Norman almost knocks the vase over in his excitement and they
both have to scramble to catch it. Leaving Norman gazing into
Sally's eyes.

                         NORMAN[13] (CONT'D)
              Six.

                         SALLY
              Now get away before you do any
              damage or Mr.Grace sees you.

Norman almost skips away but can't resist turning his head
for one last word.

                         NORMAN[13]
              Six!

And promptly walks into a pillar hoping Sally didn't notice.

                                              CUT TO:

EXT. LONDON HOTEL - REAR - 1928 - EVENING

Norman[13], in his Sunday best, is pacing up and down outside
the rear entrance to the hotel waiting for Sally. He's
kicking stones in the street, hands in pockets and looking
very nervous. He repeatedly checks his money in his pocket
and makes sure he puts it away safely. Sally appears.

                    NORMAN[13]
          Hello Sally. I'm here.

                    SALLY
          I'm not blind. Come on let's go.

Sally walks on and Norman[13] follows.

                                              CUT TO:

INT. CINEMA - 1928

Only the light from the screen and the sound of a NEWSREEL
PLAYING. Norman[13] moves in the dark along the back row to
the annoyance of the couples seated who all have to unravel
themselves to allow him to pass.

                    NORMAN[13]
          Sorry. Excuse me. Sorry...

Half way across he realises Sally isn't following him. She's
heading for a seat nearer the front. Norman[13] half-shouts
and then quiet.

                    NORMAN[13] (CONT'D)
          Sally! Sorry. Sal..

Norman[13] disturbs everyone again to get out. Sitting on a
woman's lap, treading on toes. Sally passes through the row
with ease and sits down and Norman[13] fights his way through
to sit next to her.

                    NORMAN[13] (CONT'D)
          Sal--

                    SALLY
          Shsss, it's starting.

The sound of the MOVIE STARTING.

Norman[13] slowly tries to put his arm around Sally who's having none of it and wriggles her shoulder to make his arm move. Norman[13] reluctantly settles down resting his head on his hand to watch the movie.

DISSOLVE TO:

INT. CINEMA - 1928 - LATER

The sound of the MOVIE ENDING.

The lights come up. Norman[13] is asleep with his head on his hand. Sally knocks his elbow which slips from the arm of the chair and he quickly wakes. The stand and leave the row.

                    NORMAN[13]
          That was good wasn't it?

Sally is not pleased.

                    SALLY
          Where are you taking me for supper
          Norman? I'm feeling rather peckish.

                    NORMAN[13]
          Oh, leave it to me.

Norman[13] lets Sally go ahead and he sneaks his money from his pocket and quickly counts it to make sure he has enough.

CUT TO:

INT. LONDON GRUBBY CAFE - 1928 - LATER

Norman[13] and Sally are seated at a basic table. Sally unimpressed as a waitress drops two plates of Egg and Chips in front of them and Norman[13] dips a chip in Sally's egg.

DISSOLVE TO:

INT. LONDON HOTEL - 1928 - NEXT DAY

The next day, Norman is fiddling around trying to look busy in the lobby again waiting to see Sally. When she finally appears Norman[13] rushes over.

                    NORMAN[13]
          Hello Sally. Last night was good,
          wasn't it?

                         SALLY
          Norman?

                         NORMAN[13]
          Yes Sally.

                         SALLY
          Would you do me a favour?

                         NORMAN[13]
          Anything for you Sally.

She takes a moment. Norman[13] hangs on her words.

                         SALLY
                    (deliberate)
          Don't ever speak to me again.

                         NORMAN[13]
          But Sal..

Sally simply raises a finger to his mouth. A beat and she
walks away. Before a sudden look of angry determination comes
over his face and he marches off.

                                        DISSOLVE TO:

INT. LONDON HOTEL - 1928 - LATER

Joe is busy polishing the brass on the lift when he's
surprised by Norman[13] in his own clothes and carrying a
small bag.

                         JOE
          Norm? What you doin'..?

                         NORMAN[13]
          I've done it. I couldn't wait any
          longer. I'm ready when you are.

                         JOE
          Done it? Done what?

                         NORMAN[13]
          I've told Grace where he can stick
          his job. I'm going to be a coal
          miner, in Wales!

Joe almost convulses.

                         JOE
          You've done what? Are you mental?

                    NORMAN[13]
          We're going to Wales aren't we?

                    JOE
          We? You didn't mention me did you?

                    NORMAN[13]
          Well no, but, we..

                    JOE
          That was two days ago Norm. I've
          been to bed since then and I
          haven't had chance to finalise my
          plans yet. I'm not ready to leave.

Confusion from them both.

                    NORMAN[13]
          But you said...

Joe throws his hands in the air, on his head and over his
mouth. He almost spins around total panic.

                    JOE
          Oh my God. What have you done?

Confusion as they both try to grasp the situation.

                    JOE (CONT'D)
          You better go Norm, I don't want
          Grace seeing you talking to me.

                    NORMAN[13]
          I better go?

                    JOE
          Yes. Go, go.

Joe gets inside the lift and closes the door on Norman[13]
and holds it shut as Norman[13] carries on talking.

                    NORMAN[13]
          I'm going to be a coal miner and
          nothing's going to stop me! Which
          way's Cardiff?

He doesn't wait for a reply and marches off.

                                        CUT TO WHITE:

                                        FADE IN:

EXT. CARDIFF DOCKS - 1928 - DAY - FIVE WEEKS LATER

SUPERIMPOSE: "Five weeks later, Cardiff Docks, 1928."

Norman[13] almost worn out examines the holes in his shoes and then trudges along and approaches a couple of workers standing near a hut and burning wood in a brazier.

                                                    CUT TO:

EXT. CARDIFF DOCKS - CONTINUOUS

The DOCK LABOURER#1 and DOCK LABOURER#2 are laughing.

                    DOCK LABOURER#1
            You've done what?

The labourer is incredulous and amused.

                    DOCK LABOURER#2
            You've walked for nothing. There's
            no work here. Pits are laying off
            not hiring.

                    DOCK LABOURER#1
            Walk straight home Lad. Your shoes
            might just hold out.

They laugh. Norman[13]'s disappointment is clear.

                    NORMAN[13]
            Are there any jobs going round
            here?

                    DOCK LABOURER#1
            Kid if there were any jobs going we
            wouldn't be standing here drinking
            tea would we?

Norman[13]'s exhaustion is clearly visible. Another man, REED, a big rough chinned Northerner has heard the commotion.

                    REED
            Hold up kid. What's your name?

                                                    CUT TO:

INT. SHIP MAINDY COURT - CABIN

Norman[13] has been shown below deck and allocated a bunk in a small cabin shared with the STEWARD, who doesn't look too pleased when Reed deposits Norman[13] in his cabin.

                    REED
         Here Wizzie lad, get some rest. We
         leave at first thing tomorrow.

Norman[13] tests out the bunk tentatively before slipping off
his shoes and rolling over to quickly fall into a deep sleep.

                                        DISSOLVE TO:

INT. SHIP MAINDY COURT - CABIN - NEXT MORNING

The morning comes and Norman[13]'s eyes open and the cabin
and its contents move up and down, up and down. He closes
them again to stop the motion. Just as he opens them for a
second time the face of the Steward is there briefly before a
fist comes down.

                    STEWARD
         The only cargo we carry is wheat
         and beef and you ain't either so
         get up and get to it! They got need
         of you in the galley.

Norman[13] stands, holds back the tears with hands over his
face and runs out of the cabin.

                                        CUT TO:

INT. SHIP MAINDY COURT - PASSAGEWAY - CONTINUOUS

Norman[13] comes out of his cabin straight into Reed.

                    REED
         Wow, slow down Wizzie. You don't
         have to be that keen to get to
         work, you'll give us all a bad
         name.

Reed notices Norman[13] face is marked.

                    REED (CONT'D)
         Hold up, what's happened?

                    NORMAN[13]
         I slipped.

                    REED
         Did you now? I see. Well you run
         along and mind you don't slip
         again. You'll find the galley as
         far as you can go down there. Go
         on!

When Norman[13] has gone Reed enters the Steward's cabin closing the door behind him.

The sound of MUTED VOICES, a SCUFFLE and a THUD.

                                        CUT TO:

INT. SHIP MAINDY COURT - GALLEY

The ship rises up and down. Norman[13] sits in a corner of the galley on a box peeling potatoes.

DEMITRI the Greek ship's cook in grubby whites drops another bucket in front of Norman and takes the peeled ones away. The ship, the box, the potatoes and Norman[13] rise up and down. Norman[13] looks ill.

                                        CUT TO:

EXT. SHIP MAINDY COURT - OPEN DECKS - LATER

SUPERIMPOSE: "The North Atlantic 1928."

The seas are rough. A zombie like Norman[13] throws a bucket of potato peel over the side. The wind blows them all back in to his face, covering him head to foot in peelings. Without a word, he drags himself off decorated by potato peelings.

                                        DISSOLVE TO:

INT. SHIP MAINDY COURT - OPEN DECKS - WEEKS LATER

A stretch of nice weather and calm seas. Norman[13] sits on deck peeling spuds. He watches, while some of the crew led by Reed, are hitting a punch bag hanging nearby.

                    REED
          Come on lad. Have a bash.

Norman hold up a spud.

                    NORMAN[13]
          I've got to finish these.

                    REED
          Five minutes won't hurt. Show us
          what you can do. Come on.

Norman[13] goes over and pulls on set of gloves that look almost as big him and hits the bag hard with both hands a few times swirling like a mad man.

                    REED (CONT'D)
          Wow, slow down. You've got a punch
          all right. But try this.

Reed shows Norman[13] how to make a typical boxing stance.
and moves in slow motion to demonstrate.

                    REED (CONT'D)
          Take your time. If you throw a jab,
          step in with it. Then when you
          throw a hook turn your hand and
          rotate your back foot. Like this.

Norman[13] tries it a few times and he's got it.

                    REED (CONT'D)
          That's it. You've got it. Get every
          last bit of power from your legs
          down those arms.

                                        DISSOLVE TO:

MONTAGE - SHIP MAINDY COURT - TRAINING

- Running up steps, boxing,

- Serving food, boxing,

- Delivering tea, boxing,

- Polishing brass, boxing,

- Peeling spuds. Not boxing.

END OF MONTAGE

INT. SHIP MAINDY COURT - OPEN DECKS - WEEKS LATER

Norman[13] comes on deck to dispose of more peelings. He sees
some of the crew and Reed, gathered at the side of the ship,
looking at something.

                    NORMAN[13]
          What is it?

                    REED
          Terra Firma.

                    NORMAN[13]
          Terra what..?

                    REED
          Solid ground mate. Look out
          Argentina. The Maindy Court is in
          town tonight.

The men have a laugh. Norman[13] draws back his bucket of
peelings ready to throw over the side.

                ALL CREW MEMBERS
          Wow, No, No Wizzie! Aft!

He stops in time.

                    REED
          Not against the wind lad.

                   NORMAN[13]
          Oh, yes, sorry!

Norman[13] trundles past them to dispose of the peelings and
the men discus something. When Norman[13] returns..

                    REED
          Eh, lad. We've got a proposition
          for you.

                   NORMAN[13]
          What's that?

                    REED
          In no time now we'll all be ashore.

                   NORMAN[13]
          It's OK I can stay and look after
          the ship if you want?

                    REED
          Well thank you lad that's very
          kind. The unfortunates will stay
          behind for that purpose. It was
          something else I had in mind.

                   NORMAN[13]
          Okay?

Reed leans in and speaks in lowered tones.

                    REED
          As your are now a qualified
          proponent of the noble art..

                   NORMAN[13]
          I am?

                         REED
          Boxing.. You're good at it.

The other crew members are chipping in with reassuring sounds
and acknowledging nods.

                         NORMAN[13]
          Oh, thanks. It's fun.

A few little punches in the air from Norman[13].

                         REED
          It is that. Well, this is the
          point, we know a place where they
          have a regular prize fight. Just a
          bit of fun like you say.

                         NORMAN[13]
          Prizes?

                         REED
          Money lad. And we can all use a bit
          more of that can't we?

Norman[13] nods.

                         REED (CONT'D)
          Well? What do you think.

                         NORMAN[13]
          Yes, definitely.

The men look relieved.

                         NORMAN[13] (CONT'D)
          You'll win. I know you will. They
          can't be any better than you.

                         REED
          No. No, lad, I'm saying you fight.

                         NORMAN[13]
          Me?

                         REED
          Yes, you.

                         NORMAN[13]
          I don't think I'm ready to fight
          for money.

                         REED
          All you have to do is what I taught
          you. Keep moving.
                              (MORE)

                    REED (CONT'D)
         You stay on your feet three short
         rounds and we win all win a fiver.
         How does that sound?

Norman[13] considers, then..

                    NORMAN[13]
         Nah, I don't think I'm up to that
         standard yet thanks.

Disappointment all round but Reed takes it in his stride.

                    REED
         Ok, lad. No problem. Look, we're
         going anyway so just come along and
         watch the fights. You deserve a day
         off like the rest of us.

                    NORMAN[13]
         Just come and watch?

                    REED
         Absolutely.

                                        CUT TO:

INT. ARGENTINEAN FAIRGROUND TENT - 1928 - LATER

The CROWD ROARS. Norman[13] is in the boxing ring and he's
taking a beating.

In slow motion a boxing glove connects with Norman[13]'s face
distorting his features and sending his head reeling
backwards as blood and sweat fly. He's dazed and tripping
around the ring trying to avoid a crazed Argentinean fighter.

A massive punch sends Norman[13] reeling back on the ropes.
He's trapped and the Argentinean is raining punches left and
right. Reed raises a towel in his hand but another man grabs
his hand and pulls it down. The fight continues then, saved
by the BELL, DING, DING. Norman[13] staggers to his corner
and drops to the stool.

                                        CUT TO:

INT. ARGENTINEAN FAIRGROUND TENT - 1928 - CONTINUOUS

Water splashed on Norman[13] and a towel waved up and down.

                    REED
         You're killing him lad!

                    NORMAN[13]
         Can you let him know?

                    REED
         You're doing fine. This is the last
         round, just stay away from him.

The BELL rings, DING, DING.

Reed throws Norman[13] out again who tries to avoid the
crazed Argentinean. Norman[13] receives another almighty
punch that sends him reeling back on to the ropes.

                    REED (CONT'D)
         No! Keep away lad!

Norman[13] springs straight back up and manages to land a
punch that dazes the Argentinean causing him to slow up. Reed
can't believe what he's seen.

                    REED (CONT'D)
              (excited)
         You've got him lad.

Norman[13] stands back and the Argentinean starts to recover.

                    REED (CONT'D)
         What you waiting for? Get stuck in.
         Go for it. Now!

                    NORMAN[13]
         You said stay away. I wish you'd
         make your mind up.

Norman[13] takes his chance and delivers a second and third.
The Argentinean is cut above the eye and blood trickles down.
Norman ducks and dives and lands another and another. The
Argentinean is surprised and raises his guard higher than he
has needed to before and goes into a defensive mode stepping
backwards as Norman[13] advances. The Argentinean defends
himself in the corner of the ring as Norman[13] rains blows
on him, left and right.

A hand hovers over the bell for a second that seems like an
eternity. Finally the BELL RINGS time on the final round and
Norman[13]'s corner rush the ring and raise him aloft.

The Argentinean isn't celebrating. He wipes the blood from
his face onto his glove and then gives Norman an
acknowledging nod. Norman[13] is carried away and deposited
outside the dressing room.

Norman[13] goes triumphantly into the dressing room as his shipmates carry on celebrating outside.

                                        DISSOLVE TO:

INT. ARGENTINEAN FAIRGROUND TENT - 1928 - LATER

Norman[13] emerges, all smiles, the tent is empty other than a man sweeping up. Norman[13]'s ship mates have left him.

                                        DISSOLVE TO:

INT. THE MAINDY COURT - 1928 - GALLEY

A battered, bruised and tired Norman[13] stumbles back onboard an almost deserted ship. One who has stayed is Demitri the cook who has spent his day drinking and is feeling sorry for Norman[13] and has made him a sandwich.

                    DEMITRI
          Here boy. What happened? You did
          the prize fight after all? Or
          someone rob you?

                    NORMAN[13]
          Both. But thanks Demitri. I need
          this. This is nothing. You should
          see the other fella.

Demitri still holding a bottle puts his arm around Norman[13], which makes him start to feel a bit uneasy.

                    DEMITRI
          Oh, Norman, how could they do it to
          you? You such a pretty boy too.

                    NORMAN[13]
          I'm not pretty Demitri. Men aren't
          pretty. Men are handsome but I
          don't think I'm that either.

Demitri's takes a swig from the bottle and his arm is squeezing a bit tighter.

                    DEMITRI
          Oh, no, Norman you are very pretty
          boy.

Norman[13] tries to struggle free.

                    NORMAN[13]
          Demitri what are you doing?

                    DEMITRI
Can I kiss you Norman?

                    NORMAN[13]
   What?

Norman[13] pulls lose and Demitri is trying to grab him.

                  NORMAN[13] (CONT'D)
   On yer bike mate!

A chase ensues as Norman[13] runs around the galley with
Demitri close behind.

                    DEMITRI
   Come here Norman. It's lonely
   onboard. We can be good friends.

Norman[13] shouts the only thing he knows will bring the
remaining crew running.

                    NORMAN[13]
   Man overboard! Man overboard!

Reed comes in and deals Demitri a knock out blow. Demitri is
on the floor dazed and Norman[13] can catch his breath. Reed
holds Norman[13]'s chin with his large hand and takes a look
at his bruises.

                    REED
   You've had a busy day lad. Let's
   find you a steak.

                    NORMAN[13]
   A steak? I just had a sandwich.

                    REED
   For that eye, not to eat. I don't
   think Demitri will mind.

Reed picks up a large piece of steak that Demitri had been
preparing and throws it to Norman[13].

                    REED (CONT'D)
   Here you go champ, hold that on.
   There has to be some advantage
   being on a cargo ship loaded with
   Argentinian Beef!

Norman[13] presses it to his cheek.

                    NORMAN[13]
   Where did you all get to?

Reed doesn't want to discuss that.

                    REED
                (embarrassed)
          The men got distracted lad. It
          happens to sailors who ain't got
          their head on straight. Women and
          drink. Not a good combination. We
          can only hope the majority make it
          back for the morning tides because
          The Maindy Court waits for no man
          and we'll be home for Christmas.

                    NORMAN[13]
          Will you be on the next trip?

                    REED
          We've got 7000 miles of open sea
          between us and home. Never
          underestimate that. But God willing
          I suppose I will. There ain't much
          for the likes of me ashore,
          Christmas or not. Well, part from
          women and drink. What about you?
          You thought what adventure you
          might have next after giving them
          Argentinians a beating?

                    NORMAN[13]
          I think I'm like you. Nothing much
          for me ashore either.

                    REED
          No lad, you ain't like me. And you
          can thank the lord for that. A
          young lad like you, you must have
          someone? Anyone you could be with
          at Christmas?

No answer.

                    REED (CONT'D)
          No one? No parents?

                    NORMAN[13]
          Yea, course. I'm just not sure
          where they are, that's all.

                    REED
          When we get back you find 'em out.
          They've got to be concerned.

Norman[13] not convinced. Reed tries to reassure him.

                              REED (CONT'D)
                    They'll be pleased to see you and
                    to know you're safe. It's Christmas
                    after all.

Norman[13] nods.

                                        DISSOLVE TO:

EXT. CARDIFF STREETS - 1928 - EVENING

SUPER: "Christmas 1928."

It's Christmas, the streets are full of lights, decorations
and people celebrating. Norman[13] is now a confident boy. He
pulls his coat tight and makes his way alone through the
crowded streets.

                                        DISSOLVE TO:

EXT. LONDON STREET - 1928 - SOME DAYS LATER

Norman[13] is outside a house. He takes a deep breath.

                                        CUT TO:

EXT. LONDON HOUSE - 1928 - CONTINUOUS

He knocks the door. Nothing. After a moment he reaches up to
knock again but the door starts to open. There is an
attractive YOUNG LADY holding a baby.

                         YOUNG LADY
                    Hello?

Norman[13] takes off his cap.

                         NORMAN[13]
                    Oh, hello Miss. I was looking for
                    Frederick Wisdom. Senior?

                         YOUNG LADY
                    Fred's not here. Who are you?

                         NORMAN[13]
                    I'm Norman.

Nothing.

                         NORMAN[13] (CONT'D)
                    He's my Dad.

>   YOUNG LADY
>   (shocked)
>   Oh, I see. I'm really sorry, he
>   won't be back for quite a while.

>   NORMAN[13]
>   Okay. Thank you.

The disappointment on Norman[13]'s face is clear to see. He
starts to turn and walk away.

>   YOUNG LADY
>   Why don't you come in and wait?

Norman[13] stops, pleased. He goes inside.

>   CUT TO:

INT. LONDON HOUSE - FRONT ROOM - 1928 - CONTINUOUS

Norman[13] gripping his cap. They sit in awkward silence,
except for a CLOCK TICKING loudly. Finally..

>   YOUNG LADY
>   Can I get you anything to drink.?

>   NORMAN[13]
>   A glass of water would be nice.

She hurries away and Norman[13] waits alone.

>   DISSOLVE TO:

INT. LONDON HOUSE - FRONT ROOM -1928 - MUCH LATER

The CLOCK still TICKS and now an empty glass is on a table
and the light from the window has faded to darkness.

In the hallway Norman[13] hears the DOOR RATTLE, OPEN and
CLOSE. There are MUFFLED VOICES which then stop.

The door to the front room opens abruptly and the large
shadow of Norman's Dad fills the opening. Nothing is said so
Norman states the obvious.

>   NORMAN[13]
>   Dad? It's me. Norman.

A slight pause from Norman[13] but not from his Dad.

>   NORMAN'S DAD
>   Get out!

                    NORMAN[13]
          Da..

Norman[13] stands and in a speechless daze walks out past his
father. Norman[13] hold his head high and the tears in.

                                        CUT TO:

EXT. LONDON STREET - CONTINUOUS

Norman[13] in a daze, pushes through the busy streets
knocking in to passers-by, his head is swimming, no focus.
Unable to walk any more he turns into a quiet side street.
Leans against a wall before dropping to his knees and crying.

                                     DISSOLVE TO:

EXT. LONDON STREET - 1928 - EARLY MORNING - SOME DAYS LATER

Norman[13] seated and huddled inside his coat as customers of
a food vendor come and go. A group of Soldiers, laughing and
joking walk away with their breakfasts. Norman[13] checks his
pockets for the last of his change and walks over.

The STALL OWNER, a tall man with a moustache dressed in a
white overall, is ready to serve. Norman[13] places down his
small collection of coins.

                    NORMAN[13]
          Any chance of a Bovril for that?

The Stall Owner shakes his head. He leaves the coins on the
counter and turns away. Norman[13] starts to scoop the coins
together. The Stall Owner then places a mug of Bovril and a
meat pie on the counter.

                    STALL OWNER
          Here you go lad.

                    NORMAN[13]
          Really? Thank you.

                    STALL OWNER
          And don't forget your change.

The Stall Owner pushes the coins back towards Norman[13], who
scoops his coins back up and stores them in his pocket.

                                        CUT TO:

EXT. LONDON STREET - 1928 - A FEW MOMENTS LATER

Norman[13] is sitting on a step nearby and the Stall Owner
listens to his tale.

                    STALL OWNER
          You've drawn a bad hand by the
          sounds of it lad. And your old man
          doesn't deserve a son. No offence.

Norman[13] is still busy eating and drinking.

                    STALL OWNER (CONT'D)
          These streets are no place for a
          young lad. Get away from here. Get
          away as far as you can.

                    NORMAN[13]
          I ain't got anywhere else to go and
          you've seen what money I've got.

                    STALL OWNER
          Well, for sure, this is no life for
          any young lad.

The Stall Owner takes a beat.

                    STALL OWNER (CONT'D)
          What would you say if I told you
          there was somewhere you could have
          a roof over your head and three
          square meals a day?

                    NORMAN[13]
          I don't know anywhere like that.
          Unless you mean Prison?

                    STALL OWNER
          No lad. Not prison. Take the King's
          Shilling?

                    NORMAN[13]
          The King wont give me anything?
          (Beat) Would he?

                    STALL OWNER
          Well, in a round about way, maybe
          he will. When you take The King's
          Shilling, it means you join the
          army lad.

Normans[13] speaking with a full mouth.

                    NORMAN[13]
          The army?

                    STALL OWNER
          I'm proud to say I've served
          myself. Best years of my life.

The Stall Owner straightens himself up.

                    STALL OWNER (CONT'D)
          It's a grand life. See the world
          and get some discipline.

                    NORMAN[13]
          I had enough discipline thanks.

                    STALL OWNER
          Not that sort of discipline lad.
          The good sort.

Norman[13] can't imagine good discipline.

                    STALL OWNER (CONT'D)
          The army will make you a man with
          the right values... and can give
          you a trade.

                    NORMAN[13]
          Well, how old do you have to be to
          join the army then?

                    STALL OWNER
          You need to be Sixteen to die for
          King and Country.

                    NORMAN[13]
          I'm only fourteen and I don't plan
          on dieing anytime soon.

                    STALL OWNER
          The Music Corp will take a boy at
          fourteen and I don't know many who
          have died blowing on a trumpet.

                    NORMAN[13]
          I don't know anything about music.

                    STALL OWNER
          If half the bugle players I've had
          to endure are anything to go by,
          that's a prerequisite for the job.

Norman[13] lifts the mug to his face to finish off the last of his Bovril.

CUT TO WHITE:

FADE IN:

INT. INDIAN ARMY CAMP - PARADE GROUND - SEVERAL YEARS LATER

SUPERIMPOSE: "British Barracks, Lucknow, India 1932."

We transition to an older NORMAN[18].

The sun is rising. Norman[18] standing in uniform smartly on the parade ground with a TRUMPET raised to his lips. He sounds REVEILLE to wake up his comrades. Everyone is now awake. Sound of MUMBLED MOANS, ANNOYANCE and EXPLETIVES from inside the barracks. As Norman[18] walks away he places the trumpet to his lips and blows a massive raspberry.

DISSOLVE TO:

EXT. INDIAN ARMY CAMP - PARADE GROUND - LATER

The camp springs to life. Soldiers in washrooms and lining for breakfast. A group of soldiers are being put through their paces exercising and others drilling in the parade ground.

CUT TO:

INT. INDIAN ARMY CAMP - HALL - CONTINUOUS

Posters for an upcoming "Regimental Boxing Night". The hall looks more like a boxing camp. Norman[18] is punching at a bag while another young recruit, MIKE encourages him and holds the bag.

A severe looking, SERGEANT WALKER strolls past with his cane under his arm and stares menacing at Norman[18] and Mike.

                    MIKE
               (whispers)
          Don't look Norm, it's Walker.

                    NORMAN[18]
          Where?

                    MIKE
          Behind you!

Norman[18] looks.

> MIKE (CONT'D)
> I said don't...

Mike diverts attention and pretends to be talking to
Norman[18].

> MIKE (CONT'D)
> 1,2 and again. Yes, harder!

Sergeant Walker just strolls on by with a menacing glare.

> MIKE (CONT'D)
> God he hates me.

> NORMAN[18]
> Not just you Mike, he's a bad 'en.
> I know one when I see one.

> MIKE
> He's out of control. I'd buy myself
> out just to get away from him if
> there was anything to go home for.

Norman[18] thumps at the bag as they talk.

> MIKE (CONT'D)
> Three million unemployed. Don't
> seem like hardly anyone back home
> has a job any more. If I didn't
> send my folks money I don't know
> how they'd survive.

> NORMAN[18]
> Three million?

> MIKE
> "The Great Depression."

Norman[18] stops for a moment.

> NORMAN[18]
> Three million on the bread line.
> What's great about that?

Norman[18] gives one last flurry to the bag as if taking out
his frustrations.

                                        CUT TO:

INT. INDIAN ARMY CAMP - OFFICERS MESS - LATER

Norman[18] on clarinet, Mike and small band play a staid set to one last officer, asleep in a chair, in the Officer's Mess. The band are agitated but must play on. Norman[18] reaches down for a trumpet at his side. He removes the clarinet from his lips and blows an almighty NOISE.

The Officer jolts from his slumber, but Norman[18] has returned the clarinet to his lips and plays tranquil music as if nothing at all had happened. The band can hardly contain themselves. The officer, unsure what just happened, looks around, pushes himself up out of the chair and carries himself away.

As soon as he is out of sight, the band brings the piece to an early end in a flurry of bum notes and erupt in laughter. The band members start to pack away and disperse.

                                        FADE TO:

EXT. INDIAN ARMY CAMP - PARADE GROUND - NEXT DAY

The sun is rising. Mike and the other soldiers are sweltering standing in a line in full kit.

Sergeant Walker is walking the line inspecting their kit before the parade. He is always trailed by his Indian Batman who holds a large shade over him. He pulls and prods at the men's uniforms and taps them with his cane.

                    SERGEANT
          I'm told that some of you men think
          you are too important to drill?

He stops at one SOLDIER.

                    SERGEANT (CONT'D)
          Are you important soldier?

The soldier is confused, he takes a beat to answer. The Indian helper stands behind the Sergeant and shakes is head to the soldier to give him the cue to answer.

                    SOLDIER
          No Sir?

                    SERGEANT
          Correct.

He walks on.

                    SERGEANT (CONT'D)
          As your superior, I have been told
          by my superior that I must exempt
          some of you from drill because you
          are to represent this regiment in a
          forthcoming dancing, I mean boxing,
          tournament. Yes, I think that's
          what I mean.

He prods someone with his cane then walks on and stops to
face the line near to Norman[18] and Mike.

                    SERGEANT (CONT'D)
          If I speak of you, step forward.

Some hesitation, then Norman[18], Mike and a couple of others
step forward. Mike is out of luck, he steps forward right
into the Sergeant's eye line and can be seen visibly scared.

                    SERGEANT (CONT'D)
          Well here they are men. Take a good
          look at them. The chosen few. They
          who wish to escape the real work of
          being a soldier so they can prance
          and dance around a ring.

He stares menacingly close at Mike.

                    SERGEANT (CONT'D)
          I'm not sure you could box your way
          out of a paper bag.

The Indian Helper winces in anticipation.

                    MIKE
          I'm, I'm..

                    SERGEANT
          Spit it out man.

Walker puts his cane under Mike's chin and pushes his head
back. Norman[18] tries to rescue Mike.

                    NORMAN[18]
          He's in my corner Sir.

                    SERGEANT
          Is he a ventriloquist as well?

Silence. This isn't good. The Indian helper grimaces.

                    SERGEANT (CONT'D)
          If you're not boxing get your arse
          back in line.

Mike steps back leaving Walker's cane still poised where it was. Walker diverts his attention to Norman[18].

> SERGEANT (CONT'D)
> Let me be clear. You are not exempt
> from drill. For you it is merely
> delayed. Pending. And if, as I
> expect, you do not perform
> adequately at said boxing
> tournament and therefore bring
> disgrace on this regiment it will
> be my duty and indeed my pleasure
> to ensure you regret your
> inadequate performances.

He stands back and shouts to the line.

> SERGEANT (CONT'D)
> Is that clear?

> EVERYONE
> Yes Sir!

> SERGEANT
> Go to your dance. Dismissed!

Norman[18]and the boxers make their escape. The Sergeant speaks to those left behind.

> SERGEANT (CONT'D)
> His Majesty expects every man to do
> his duty. That is to drill. If
> those men can not drill, you must
> take up the slack. I will not allow
> His Majesty to be disappointed.

The look on Mike's face shows he knows what that means. Hard drill in full sun.

> SERGEANT (CONT'D)
> Attention!

The men stand to attention and the commands to march follow.

> DISSOLVE TO:

INT. INDIAN ARMY CAMP - HALL - LATER

Norman[18] punches away at the BAG to the sound off screen of the SOLDIERS DRILLING.

                    SERGEANT (O.S.)
           Left, Right, Left, Right, Left.

                                        DISSOLVE TO:

EXT. INDIAN ARMY CAMP - PARADE GROUND - CONTINUOUS

The sun starts to lower in the sky. The men are tired.

                    SERGEANT (O.S.)
           Left, Left, Left, Right, Left.

                                        DISSOLVE TO:

INT. INDIAN ARMY CAMP - BARRACK ROOM - LATER

Norman[18] is in the barrack room when, Mike and the other
soldiers come bursting back into their barracks, drenched in
sweat. Mike kicks off his boots and flops out on his bunk.
Norman[18] is in his vest and pants.

                    MIKE
           Oh, this is the life.

Norman[18] starts air boxing trying to make Mike laugh.

                    NORMAN[18]
           Come on, cheer up Mike'y. You could
           be walking the streets.

Mike sits up on the edge of his bunk and the conversation
gets a bit deep.

                    MIKE
           You love all this don't you?

                    NORMAN[18]
           Mike, I had literally nothing
           before I joined up. Now I've got my
           mates, my music and my sport. What
           more could I ask for? I'm not going
           to let Walker spoil that for me.

Norman[18] goes through his boxing moves.

                    MIKE
           Ladies and Gentlemen. In the blue
           corner boxing in, nearly, white
           vest and pants we have soon to be
           Flyweight Champion, Private Norman
           Wisdom.

The other soldiers applaud and laugh when they look over and
see Norman[18] boxing.

                    MIKE (CONT'D)
          Who you fighting Norm?

                    NORMAN[18]
          I don't know but he's a big 'un.

                    MIKE
          Seconds out round one.

Mike grabs a teaspoon and a metal mug and rings the start of
the round. DING, DING.

Norman[18] goes into a full boxing match against his
invisible opponent. One of the band PLAYS NOTES on his
TRUMPET to match Norman[18]'s punches and blows. The soldiers
cheer along.

Norman[18] throws a series of punches, ducking and diving. He
pretends to be punched and throwing his head back in a one-
two movement before an imaginary punch sends him flying
through the air. The 'audience' love it and cheer him on,
laughing and clapping. Mike rushes over.

                    MIKE (CONT'D)
          1,2,..

                                        DISSOLVE TO:

INT. INDIAN ARMY CAMP - HALL - NEXT EVENING

The CROWD ROAR. Norman[18]is fighting and down for the count.
A REFEREE counts on..

                    REFEREE
          3,4..

Norman[18] picks himself up and the Referee brushes down his
gloves and he's ready to fight on.

His rival throws a left and a right combination whichthe now
skillful Norman[18] ducks and dodges easily and returns a
body shot, setting his rival back on his feet allowing
Norman[18] to deliver an upper cut that sends him falling
back against the ropes.

Both fighters are shattered, it has been a long fight.
Norman[18]'s rival comes forward and puts everything into one
last attempt to knock Norman[18] out. He throws his biggest
right hand he can muster. Norman[18] ducks under and leaves
it to swing wildly over his head.

Then he comes up and throws another right to the man's middle and another over the top of his opponents gloves and finally a left hook sending his opponent to the canvas.

The Referee comes between them and starts his count.

                    REFEREE (CONT'D)
          1,2,3,

The rival lifts his knees from the canvas dazed and the referee takes brushes his gloves against his shirt.

The rival comes forward and throws another punch, which Norman[18] steps back from leaving his opponent off balance. Norman[18] steps forward and delivers a knock out blow. His rival is felled like a tree and collapses back to the deck. A towel comes flying in to the ring from the rival's corner and the referee waves his arms to signal the fight is over.

The crowd of soldiers erupt in celebration as Norman[18] is raised aloft eventually he is handed the prize belt which is placed around his middle.

                              DISSOLVE TO:

EXT. INDIAN ARMY CAMP - PARADE GROUND - NEXT MORNING

The Indian Sun shows itself above the horizon. Off screen the SOUND OF REVEILLE. A bruised Norman[18] doing his morning duty but wearing the prized boxing over his uniform.

                              CUT TO:

EXT. INDIAN ARMY CAMP - PARADE GROUND - LATER

Norman[18] (slightly bruised facially), Mike and the other soldiers are on parade in the full Indian sun. The Sergeant is walking the ranks tailed by his Indian Batman and shielded from the sun. He prods soldiers with his cane where he sees their uniform unbuttoned or not clean. He get's to where Mike and Norman[18] are in the line and stops at Mike.

                    SERGEANT
          Lad, why have you bought a shovel
          on parade?

                    MIKE
          I haven't Sir?

                    SERGEANT
          This lad. Look at it.

He taps Mike's rifle with his cane.

>   SERGEANT (CONT'D)
>   There's more dirt on this rifle
>   than on this parade ground floor.

>   MIKE
>   But I cleaned it Sir.

>   SERGEANT
>   You cleaned it? I don't think so.
>   If you like dirt so much get your
>   face in it.

>   MIKE
>   Sir?

>   SERGEANT
>   (shouts)
>   Get down and give me twenty!

Mike lowers himself to the ground doing push ups. The
sergeant moves on to Norman[18].

>   SERGEANT (CONT'D)
>   I see we have royalty in our midst.

Norman[18] keeps his eyes front.

>   SERGEANT (CONT'D)
>   A lucky punch will buy you no
>   favours on my parade ground laddie.

>   NORMAN[18]
>   Sir.

>   SERGEANT
>   (to Mike)
>   Enough.

Mike rejoins the ranks, hot and bothered.

>   SERGEANT (CONT'D)
>   Soldier, you bring a dirty rifle on
>   my parade ground again and I..

>   MIKE
>   Sir.

There's a slight pause of anticipation before the orders come
out loud and fierce. The sergeant puffs up his chest. The
words are individual and mostly stretched out so far they are
hardly recognisable.

                    SERGEANT
          Left face.

The soldiers all obey.

                    SERGEANT (CONT'D)
          By the Left. Quick march.
          Left. Left. Left, right. Left.

They march the parade ground.

                    SERGEANT (CONT'D)
          Keep up at the rear. Would you like
          us to slow down for you?

The sun beats down on them while the Sergeant stays under the
shade barking his orders.

                    MIKE
               (quiet)
          Norm. I can't take this!

                    NORMAN[18]
               (whispers)
          You can, just march?

                    MIKE
          I can't. It's 100 degrees out here,
          I nearly died the other day. I
          can't do it again.

                    NORMAN[18]
          If Walker knows you're flagging
          he'll have you.

                    MIKE
          I can't Norm.

Norman[18] realises he has to do something. He waits a few
steps and then trips himself up, stumbling into the soldier
in front of him. Everyone is falling over themselves and each
other and the parade is ruined.

                    SERGEANT
          Stop it! Stop it! Halt!

The Sergeant runs over followed by his Indian Batman.

                    SERGEANT (CONT'D)
          What are you doing? You don't
          deserve the uniforms on your backs.
          Get yourselves to attention!

The soldiers scramble to collect themselves and finally stand
to attention. The Sergeant towers over Norman[18].

> SERGEANT (CONT'D)
> What happened Wisdom?

> NORMAN[18]
> Sorry Sir. It's difficult Sir.

> SERGEANT
> Difficult? What exactly is so
> bloody difficult man? You can walk
> can't you?

> NORMAN[18]
> Yes Sir.

> SERGEANT
> Well, I'm just asking you to do
> that - but without falling down? Do
> you think that's a possibility?

> NORMAN[18]
> Yes Sir. It's just...

Norman[18] stops himself speaking.

> SERGEANT
> (sarcastic)
> Oh no, please don't stop Wisdom.
> Carry on. We're all ears. What were
> you going to say?

> SERGEANT (CONT'D)
> You all want to hear what Wisdom
> has to say don't you?

No answer.

> SERGEANT (CONT'D)
> (shouts)
> Don't you?

> EVERYONE
> Yes Sir.

Even the Indian Batman seems interested.

> SERGEANT
> (patronising)
> Off you go lad. We are all hanging
> on your every word.

The Sergeant fakes extreme interest and sympathy.

NORMAN[18]
Well... it's..

SERGEANT
Come on lad you're amongst friends.
Spit it out. I can hardly wait.

NORMAN[18]
I wasn't sure what you were going
to say next Sir.

SERGEANT
Pardon?

The Sergeant almost hyperventilates. He can't believe his
ears. He looks around hardly knowing what to say.

SERGEANT (CONT'D)
Left, Right, Left, Right, and you
didn't know what was coming next?

Norman[18] shrugs acknowledgment. The Sergeant's frustration
finds new levels.

NORMAN[18]
Well, I was thinking the order to
left wheel was coming and I was
getting ready. But it didn't come..
And while I was thinking about that
I tripped.

Silence except for few sniggers from the soldiers.

SERGEANT
(incredulous)
Is that it? Have you finished?

NORMAN[18]
Yes Sir.

SERGEANT
(quiet)
So all this mayhem is caused
because you were thinking?

Silence but Norman[18] nods a gesture of acknowledgement.

SERGEANT (CONT'D)
(loud)
You Wisdom, are a fool!

SERGEANT (CONT'D)
(calm)
You're in the army now.
(MORE)

                    SERGEANT (CONT'D)
          No need to think. All you have to
          do is follow the instructions I
          give, when I give them. Let your
          superiors do the thinking for you.

Norman[18] sort of shake of the head. This is like a red flag
to a bull.

                    SERGEANT (CONT'D)
          What are you trying to say Wisdom?

                    NORMAN[18]
          Well.. It's easy for you because
          you know what's coming next.

Sniggers intensify. The Sergeant is frustrated.

                    SERGEANT
          Right, call out your orders Wisdom.

                    NORMAN[18]
          What?

                    SERGEANT
          You heard me. You call out the
          orders I will show you how easy it
          is to obey.

                    NORMAN[18]
          I can't do that.

                    SERGEANT
          That's an order!

                    NORMAN[18]
          Oh, well.. All right then.

It's going much better than even Norman planned. The Sergeant
places himself to attention, ready and waiting.

                    NORMAN[18] (CONT'D)
          Attention!

Out of the corner of his mouth..

                    SERGEANT
          I'm already at attention.

                    NORMAN[18]
          Oh, yes. Right.

Norman walks to the other side of the Sergeant. He
tentatively reaches to take the cane the Sergeant keeps under
his arm with a slight tug.

The Sergeant is reluctant to releases it. Norman[18] gives it a harder pull and it's his. He places it under his arm and walks around with the cane getting in to his new role.

The Indian Batman puts his shade over Norman's head.

           NORMAN[18] (CONT'D)
Le..

The Sergeant twitches ready to move.

           NORMAN[18] (CONT'D)
No... Hang on. Hang on.... No
cheating. Wait for it...!

           NORMAN[18] (CONT'D)
     (slow, then very fast)
Le... left Face.

The Sergeant spins to his left.

           NORMAN[18] (CONT'D)
By the Left.

The Sergeant is chomping at the bit to start.

           NORMAN[18] (CONT'D)
Quick march.

The Sergeant starts marching. But Norman[18] swaps his commands and calls out Left when the Sergeant is striding Right, and Right when he is striding Left. Confusing him.

           NORMAN[18] (CONT'D)
Left, Left, Left.

The Sergeant skips to bring his marching step in line. The commands get harder and faster and Norman[18]'s impression of the Sergeant becomes more and more intense and accurate.

           NORMAN[18] (CONT'D)
Double time, Quick March. Left.
Left. Left, Right. Left. Left
Wheel, left.

This carries on a for while and the sweat is now dripping from the Sergeant's brow but Norman[18] keeps him going calling out more orders in rapid time. Finally the Sergeant has completed a lap of the parade ground and returned back to Norman[18] and the rest of the troop.

           NORMAN[18] (CONT'D)
Halt! Stand at ease.

The Sergeant now dripping sweat snatches back his cane from Norman[18]. He hides his tiredness.

> SERGEANT
> There! That Wisdom is how it is
> done. Do you see that?

> NORMAN[18]
> Yes Sir. Thank you Sir.

The Sergeant is far too hot now to carry on. He's exhausted but doesn't want it to show. The Indian Batman is still shielding Norman[18].

> SERGEANT
> Right, Dismissed!
> (to the batman)
> And put that bloody thing over me.

Everyone rushes away before he has time to change his mind.

> CUT TO:

INT. INDIAN ARMY CAMP - OFFICERS MESS - THAT EVENING

Norman[18], Mike, and the band are playing their standard set. The audience, as usual ignoring them.

They finish the piece to no applause just the incessant chatter and joviality of the Officers who don't even realise the music has stopped.

> MIKE
> What do you want to play now? Not
> that it matters.

Norman[18] stands.

> MIKE (CONT'D)
> (whispered)
> Norm? What you doing?

Norman[18] stands and starts singing a ballad. The noise stops and the officers turn. Everyone in stunned silence before Mike starts playing along. Then the other band members join in one by one. Norman gains confidence and his song and dance routine captures everyone's attention and when it's finished the whole room rise to applaud.

> MIKE (CONT'D)
> They love you Norm.

Normans[18] soaks it up.

CUT TO WHITE:

FADE IN:

INT. LONDON FISH AND CHIP SHOP - 1938

SUPERIMPOSE: "London, 1938."

Newspaper headline reads "Chamberlain to meet Hitler." Before it's wrapped around a portion of Fish and Chips.

We transition to an older NORMAN[21] waiting to be served. DOREEN a young girl behind the counter hands Norman[21] his packet of fish and chips.

> DOREEN
> There you go.

She doesn't let go.

> DOREEN (CONT'D)
> You're a regular now aren't you.

> NORMAN[21]
> Yes. I work at the telephone
> exchange around the corner.

> DOREEN
> Oh, right.

> NORMAN[21]
> But, I'm an entertainer really.

> DOREEN
> Oh? Will I have heard of you?

> NORMAN[21]
> (shy)
> Don't think so. I'm Norman.

> DOREEN
> I'm Doreen.

> NORMAN[21]
> Hello Doreen.

> DOREEN
> Hello Norman.

Behind Norman[21] is a CUSTOMER waiting to be served.

                    CUSTOMER
                 (timidly)
            Portion of chips please?

Doreen and Norman[21] are oblivious.

                    CUSTOMER (CONT'D)
                 (quiet)
            Chips?

                    NORMAN[21]
            We could go out for a stroll
            sometime? Just because we both work
            evenings.. You know.

                    DOREEN
            Oh. I think I'd like that.

Norman[21] takes control of the fish and chip package and
glides out of the shop in a bit of a daze.

                    CUSTOMER
            Chips. And he didn't pay for those.

Doreen is flustered.

                                        DISSOLVE TO:

EXT. LONDON CHURCH - 1939 - SOME MONTH'S LATER - DAY

The BELLS RING as Norman[21] and Doreen come out of their
wedding ceremony to a small crowd to be showered with rice.

                                        CUT TO:

INT. LONDON FLAT - KITCHEN - CONTINUOUS

SUPERIMPOSE: "London, 3rd September 1939."

Norman[21] and Doreen are sitting around a kitchen table
listening to the RADIO. CHAMBERLAIN addresses the nation.

                    CHAMBERLAIN (V.O.)
            This morning the British Ambassador
            in Berlin handed the German
            government a final note stating
            that unless we heard from them by
            11 O'clock that they were prepared
            at once to withdraw their troops
            from Poland a state of war would
            exist between us.

Norman[21] and Doreen hold hands.

> CHAMBERLAIN (V.O.)
> I have to tell you now that no such
> undertaking has been received and
> consequently this country is at war
> with Germany.

Norman[21] turns OFF the RADIO.

> DOREEN
> Will they call you up? You being an
> ex-soldier an all.

> NORMAN[21]
> No. Don't worry. It'll all be over
> by Christmas. And the telephone
> exchange is a protected occupation.
> So we'll be fine. I promise.

Norman[21] comforts Doreen. While his thoughts are elsewhere.

> DISSOLVE TO:

MONTAGE - BOMBING CAMPAIGNS - 1940'S

- Newsreel footage

- Bombing raids and devastation

- The blitz

- Rubble and destruction

END MONTAGE

> DISSOLVE TO:

INT. LONDON TELEPHONE EXCHANGE - 1942

A half hanging sign on the wall says "TELEPHONE EXCHANGE".
Workers putting tape on broken windows and installing
blackout materials.

Norman[21] is walking past an office. The door opens
abruptly. A small busy man, MR. JEFERRIES, comes out and
almost bumps into Norman[21].

                    MR. JEFERRIES
          Ah, you. You're ....?

                    NORMAN[21]
          Wisdom, Sir.

                    MR. JEFERRIES
          How long have you worked here
          Wisdom?

                    NORMAN[21]
          About three years now Mr Jeferries.

                    MR. JEFERRIES
          Excellent. I am relieving you of
          your duties with immediate effect.

                    NORMAN[21]
               (shocked)
          What?

Mr Jeferries hands Norman[21] a folded piece of paper.

                    MR. JEFERRIES
          You will instead report to this
          address and you will not tell
          anyone where you have gone or what
          you are doing there.

                    NORMAN[21]
          I.?

                    MR. JEFERRIES
          Do you understand?

                    NORMAN[21]
          Yes. I understand. I think?

                    MR. JEFERRIES
          Then no time to lose. Off you go.

                                        CUT TO:

EXT. LONDON SECRET BUNKER - 1942 - SOME TIME LATER

SUPER: "LONDON, SECRET BUNKER, 1942."

Norman[21] walks along the bomb ravaged streets. He looks
around trying to check the location against the one written
on the paper he was given. A large green door.

He bangs on the door. No answer. So Norman[21]pushes the
door, only to find it opens, so walks inside.

As the door closes behind him a soldier carrying a rifle over his shoulder, returns to his post guarding the door.

                                        CUT TO:

INT. LONDON SECRET BUNKER - CONTINUOUS

At the top of a long flight of steps. Normans can hear some MUFFLED NOISES and TALKING coming from below so tentatively he walks down and down the dark stairway.

The NOISES get louder. When he arrives at the bottom he is in a secret communications bunker heaving with soldiers and men and women rushing. Some are using long poles to push tank shaped models around a map on a large table. Radio operators with headsets talking and receiving communications.

Nonsensical verbal commands are being shouted out across the room and received with equally nonsensical replies.

Norman[21] looks around, open mouthed. Before he can take another step two large soldiers rush to him. They scoop him off his feet, legs kicking as they drag him to one side.

                    NORMAN[21]
          Here hang on! What's your game?
          There's a letter in my pocket.
          Check my pocket.

Norman[21] is making a fuss, but as he's being carried away,

Across the room the unmistakable figure of WINSTON CHURCHILL, at his side stands a young lady, his PERSONAL ASSISTANT nodding attentively.

                    NORMAN[21] (CONT'D)
               (shock)
          Here. That's...? Blimey.

                    WINSTON CHURCHILL
          What is all the commotion?

An ARMY OFFICER rushes forward to deal with the incident.

                    ARMY OFFICER
          Put him down. Who are you man?

They set Norman[21] back on his feet. Norman[21] retrieves the paper from his pocket.

                    NORMAN[21]
          Wisdom Sir. It's all in here.

The Army Officer reads it and nods.

>   ARMY OFFICER
>   Switchboards is it?

>   NORMAN[21]
>   Yes Sir.

>   OFFICER
>   Right follow me.

The Army Officer leads Norman[21] to a corner of the room
where a plug board telephone exchange is located. As
Norman[21] walks along he can't take his gaze from where
Winston is sitting and promptly walks into the PA who is now
coming in the opposite direction sending her papers flying on
to the floor.

>   NORMAN[21]
>   Oh Sorry.

Norman[21] picks up the papers but just shoves them crumpled
into the PA's arms.

>   OFFICER
>   Over here Wisdom. Right, you know
>   this model of exchange I take it?

Norman[21] sits down and puts on the headset.

>   NORMAN[21]
>   Yes Sir.

>   OFFICER
>   All you have to do is connect the
>   PM to whoever his PA asks for.

Norman[21] can't hear with the headset on.

>   NORMAN[21]
>   (too loud)
>   Pardon?

The Army Officer lifts off the headset from Norman[21]'s head
so he can hear.

>   OFFICER
>   (patient)
>   The PM will tell the PA and the PA
>   will tell you who the PM wants to
>   speak to. You connect them on the
>   QT. Got it?

                    NORMAN[21]
          Got it. Sir.

                    OFFICER
          Good man.

The Army Officer walks off leaving Norman[21] to it. He sits
there and waits but nothing happens. He starts to fidget,
flexing his fingers and then pushing a few papers across his
desk, tidying them up and trying to look efficient.

Norman[21] realises his chair is a newfangled swivel chair.
He realises it spins and tries it out a little, then gives
himself a mighty spin, spinning all the way round, knocking
the papers on to the floor and tangling the wire around his
neck. He spins the other direction to stop himself being
strangled and then dives down to retrieve the papers.

He pops up his head and is looking over the large table that
has the troop positions represented by small models. He
accidentally knocks one of the poles that are being used to
push the tanks and troops around map and pushes them out of
position. He realises what he has done but no one else has
noticed so he goes back to ground scooping papers together.
As he moves around he gets tangled in the wires to his
headset again and starts to choke.

Then the lights on the exchange start to flash - a call is
coming in. He struggles to reach the plugs in time, finally
managing to connect the call while still tied up with the
headphone cables.

                    NORMAN[21]
                (croaking)
          How may I connect your call?

                                        CUT TO:

INT. US COMMAND - SAME

GENERAL PATTON calling from the US.

INTERCUT.

                    GENERAL PATTON
          Patton here. Connect me to the PM.

Norman[21] is shocked and also still tied up. He just can't
reach the socket he needs to connect to.

                    NORMAN[21]
                (croaking)
          Patt? Just hold the line please.

Norman[21] stretches to try and reach the plug to connect the call. He can see Winston sitting there waiting.

> WINSTON CHURCHILL
> The Americans are late again.
> Unreliable as always.

The personal assistant realises Norman[21] is tangled. Without attracting Winston Churchill's attention she goes over and unwinds the cable from Norman[21] who is now gasping for air.

> PERSONAL ASSISTANT
> Are you all right?

Norman[21] can't speak but he nods.

> PERSONAL ASSISTANT (CONT'D)
> We're expecting an urgent call from the US.

Norman[21] holds up the end of the plug.

> NORMAN[21]
> (croaking)
> Here.

> PERSONAL ASSISTANT
> Then put it through quickly.

Norman[21] puts the plug into the socket and the PHONE by Winston Churchill starts to RING. The PA quickly goes back to answer it.

> PERSONAL ASSISTANT (CONT'D)
> Hello?

Norman[21] is now waiving at her from across the room.

> NORMAN[21]
> (croaking)
> It's me, over here.

> PERSONAL ASSISTANT
> (mouthing)
> Put the call through, quickly.

Norman[21] plugs a few more connections.

> PERSONAL ASSISTANT (CONT'D)
> (to Winston)
> Sir. General Patton on the line.

           WINSTON CHURCHILL
    Ah, about time. Late to the war and
    late for the call.

She hands over the phone to Winston.

           GENERAL PATTON
    Damn it man. We've been cut off.

           WINSTON CHURCHILL
    What? You've been cut you off?

He sees the troop positions on the large table.

           WINSTON CHURCHILL (CONT'D)
    Good grief, how did they get there?

Blank faces in the room. No one knows what has happened.

           WINSTON CHURCHILL (CONT'D)
    Issue the command to retreat.

           GENERAL PATTON (O.S.)
    Retreat? We can't retreat, we'll be
    in the sea. Have you been drinking
    man?

Next to Winston Churchill is a large glass of Brandy.

           WINSTON CHURCHILL
      (cough)
    Certainly not!

The PA rushes over to Norman[21], in a panic.

           PERSONAL ASSISTANT
    What on earth is happening?

           NORMAN[21]
    I just connected them and I think
    they've got their wires crossed.

Slight embarrassed pause.

           NORMAN[21] (CONT'D)
    .. and I may have moved those a
    bit. Does that matter?

           PERSONAL ASSISTANT
    Yes, yes I think it does. Oh no.

           NORMAN[21]
    Sorry.

                    PERSONAL ASSISTANT
          Disconnect them and I'll try and
          sort it out before we end up at war
          with the US.

Norman[21] pulls out a plug from the board.

                    WINSTON CHURCHILL
          Hello?

The line is dead.

                    GENERAL PATTON (O.S.)
          Hello?

                    NORMAN[21]
              (disguising his voice)
          How may I connect your call?

                    GENERAL PATTON (O.S.)
          I'm already on a call man. Do you
          know who this is?

                    NORMAN[21]
          No. Do you know who this is?

                    GENERAL PATTON (O.S.)
          No I don't.

                    NORMAN[21]
          Are you sure?

                    GENERAL PATTON (O.S.)
          I'm absolutely positive.

                    NORMAN[21]
          That's good.

Norman[21] pulls out the plug to disconnect him leaving him
speaking to himself.

                    GENERAL PATTON
          Hello? Hello?

On the opposite side of the room the PA is calming Winston
Churchill down who is still trying to talk on the phone,
which is now dead.

                    WINSTON CHURCHILL
          Where has that idiot gone?

                    PERSONAL ASSISTANT
          I think it's a communications issue
          Sir, some crossed wires.

Norman[21] dives on to the floor and sneaks across to the
large table with the models on. Everyone is busy, rushing
here and there and Norman[21] manages to reach over and pull
the troops back to where they should be before diving back to
the switchboard and sitting there efficiently trying to look
like nothing has happened, with his legs crossed and his
hands on his knees twiddling his crossed fingers.

                    WINSTON CHURCHILL
          Communications issues? I think
          perhaps that is the understatement
          of the War my dear. We need to deal
          with the troops urgently. They are
          a hundred miles out of position.

He gestures to the large board and the troop models now back
in the correct position.

                    WINSTON CHURCHILL (CONT'D)
          Oh, they...?

The PA passes it off without comment.

                    PERSONAL ASSISTANT
          Would you like another drink?

                    WINSTON CHURCHILL
          Ye, no, no. Perhaps not.

Winston settles back into his chair unsure of what just
happened and puffs on his cigar.

                              DISSOLVE TO:

INT. LONDON FLAT - KITCHEN - 1942

SUPERIMPOSE: "London, 1942."

Doreen sitting, cold food on the table. A coat on the chair
and suitcase packed. Sound of the FRONT DOOR OPENING and
CLOSING.

                    NORMAN[21] (O.S.)
          Doreen?

Norman[21] walks in and realises..

                    NORMAN[21] (CONT'D)
          What's wrong?

                    DOREEN
          I'm going to my mother's.

                         NORMAN[21]
           Why?

He grabs her hand.

                         DOREEN
           This came for you today.

She pushes an opened brown envelope towards him.

                         NORMAN[21]
                (quiet)
           Call up? They told me my position
           was exempt.

                         DOREEN
           Perhaps it's because you've been
           pestering the recruiting office?

                         NORMAN[21]
           I..

                         DOREEN
           You really thought I wouldn't find
           out? Every other woman's husband in
           the town trying to avoid being
           called up and mine asking where his
           papers are? You didn't think anyone
           would mention it to me?

There's nothing Norman[21] can say so there is an uneasy
silence instead.

                         DOREEN (CONT'D)
           Well you've got what you wanted.
           Just be careful for pity's sake.

She goes to leave, Norman grabs her hand.

                         NORMAN[21]
           Doreen...

                         DOREEN
                (tender)
           Norman don't fool yourself or
           torment me any more. We both know
           things haven't been right for a
           long time. You've got your dreams..

She picks up and drops the envelope.

                         DOREEN (CONT'D)
           This, is just your way to chase
           those dreams Norman.
                (MORE)

                    DOREEN (CONT'D)
          And it's clear I don't feature in
          them. So, this is best for us both.

She gently pulls her hand loose.

                    DOREEN (CONT'D)
          Have a good life Norman.

Doreen picks up her coat and case and walks out. Sound of the
DOOR CLOSING. Norman[21] picks up the envelope.

                              DISSOLVE TO:

MONTAGE - VARIOUS

WAR TIME MUSIC plays.

- The years go past

- 1943

- Norman[21] and the army band playing the circuit

- 1944

- Entertaining the troops in hospitals and barracks.

END OF MONTAGE

EXT. ARMY BARRACKS - CHELTENHAM - DAY

SUPERIMPOSE: "ARMY BARRACKS, Cheltenham, May 8th, 1945."

Norman[21] is in the yard washing down an army truck. When
suddenly nearby doors burst open and soldiers come running
from every direction.

                    SOLDIER
          It's over, it's over!

Soldiers running everywhere. Normans[21] grabs one that is
running past.

                    NORMAN[21]
          What's happened?

                    SOLDIER
          It's over! The bloody war is over.
          Germany surrendered!

                    NORMAN[21]
               (disappointed)
          When?

                    SOLDIER
          Now, right now. It's all over the
          radio. It's bloody over!

The soldier pushes loose and runs with the others. Manic
happiness all around.

                                        DISSOLVE TO:

EXT. LONDON STREETS - VE DAY

Newsreel footage of VE Day celebrations. Soldiers kissing
girls, parties, dancing in the streets and drinking.

                                        CUT TO WHITE:

                                        FADE IN:

EXT. COLLINS MUSIC HALL - 1945 - DAY

Norman[21] in Demob suit, is walking the war ravaged streets
of London with a copy of the stage newspaper. He walks in to
a theatre.

                                        CUT TO:

INT. COLLINS MUSIC HALL - MANAGERS OFFICE

The music HALL MANAGER, a typical show business shark, is
busy around his office and desk as Norman[21] pitches.

                    HALL MANAGER
          You again?

                    NORMAN[21]
          Why don't you just give me a
          chance? If I'm rubbish you'll never
          see me again.

                    HALL MANAGER
          You have got no idea how appealing
          that sounds. What's the act again?

                    NORMAN[21]
          The Successful Failure.

                    HALL MANAGER
          Ok, I'll bite. What exactly is a
          Successful Failure?

                    NORMAN[21]
          Well, it's... funny...

                    HALL MANAGER
          As long as it makes you laugh.

Norman[21] is frustrated.

                    HALL MANAGER (CONT'D)
          Look, despite what those lot out
          there will tell you, I'm not a
          naturally cruel man. But I'm
          fighting you ex-servicemen off with
          sticks since the war and, some of
          these guys actually had careers
          before they got called up. They had
          their names in lights and now
          they're fighting each other for the
          bottom of the bill.

Norman[21] knows he's right.

                    HALL MANAGER (CONT'D)
          Do us both a favour and get 9 to 5
          job? There has to be something out
          there. Even for you. But don't tell
          anyone else you're a failure –
          successful or otherwise.

                    NORMAN[21]
          No! No, look. This is what I want.
          I am experienced. I've toured with
          the army band for years in India
          and back home.

The Manager interrupts and gestures around.

                    HALL MANAGER
          Where are they then?

                    NORMAN[21]
          Who?

                    HALL MANAGER
          The rest of the band? I might be
          interested in that.

                    NORMAN[21]
          It's just me now.

                    HALL MANAGER
          The Successful Failure?

                    NORMAN[21]
          Yes, it's comedy, miming and
          singing. I fall over, things go
          wrong and I play music.

                    HALL MANAGER
                (sarcastic)
          I've got to be honest. I don't have
          anyone that falls over. That must
          have taken years of training.

                    NORMAN[21]
          Just one chance. That's all I'm
          asking for.

                    HALL MANAGER
          I've got a feeling I'll regret
          this. I'll try you on the grave
          yard slot. If you last the week
          I'll pay you £5. That's the best I
          can do. Take it or leave it!

                    NORMAN[21]
          I'll take it!

                    HALL MANAGER
          You will?

Norman[21] beams with delight.

                    HALL MANAGER (CONT'D)
          Mr Failure, before you go, would
          you have accepted three pounds? You
          would have wouldn't you?

Norman[21] pulls a small amount of money from his pockets.

                    NORMAN[21]
          This is all I have to my name. I'd
          have happily paid you every penny.
          Thank you. You won't regret it.

                    HALL MANAGER
          I already do. Go on get out before
          I change my mind.

Norman[21] leaves and shuts the door.

                                        CUT TO:

EXT. COLLINS MUSIC HALL - THE FOLLOWING WEEK

A man pastes the music hall posters to advertise the week
ahead and they show Norman[21]'s entry on the bill. The
opening act as "The Successful Failure."

                                        CUT TO:

INT. COLLINS MUSIC HALL - STAGE WINGS - LATER

A small BAND PLAYS. Norman[21] stands nervously, dressed in
his "Successful Failure" costume. An ill fitting long tails
suit with trousers much too small for even his short frame. A
dozen leggy dance girls go through the final parts of their
dance routine to an almost empty house.

The STAGE MANAGER is controlling the proceedings. The Dance
Girls come running past Norman[21] as they leave the stage..

                    STAGE MANAGER
              You're on.

                    NORMAN[21]
              You sure the band are ready?

The Stage manager is more interested in watching the leggy
girls that have just run past disappear into their dressing
rooms. Then he realises he is being spoken to.

                    STAGE MANAGER
              What? Oh, they're as ready as
              they'll ever be. That's your cue.
              Go on, break a leg.

The band strike up with Norman[21]'s music and he rushes on.

                                        CUT TO:

INT. COLLINS MUSIC HALL - STAGE - CONTINUOUS

Norman[21] runs out then comes to a standing stop on the
stage to a singular applause from somewhere in the dark. He
addresses the small band.

                    NORMAN[21]
                  (fake posh)
              If you would be so gracious.

The small band strikes up and the music for Norman[21]'s act,
"I'll Walk Beside You", starts. Norman[21] stands at the
microphone with his hands almost in a praying pose as he
alludes to this "high brow" entertainment that is to follow.

> NORMAN[21] (CONT'D)
> (singing)
> I'll walk besides you...

As Norman[21] had instructed the band is in the wrong key
leaving Norman[21] singing desperately high and struggling to
get his breath and catch up with the band.

> NORMAN[21] (CONT'D)
> No, no, it's too high. Bring it
> down, bring it down!

The audience laugh. The band stop and Norman[21] composes
himself to have another go.

> NORMAN[21] (CONT'D)
> (singing)
> I'll walk besides you...

This time the band is too low and Norman[21] has to strain to
reach the notes before giving up again.

> NORMAN[21] (CONT'D)
> Oh blimey!

He goes from one musician to the next, as part of his pre-
planned act, he tries to make them play in a the right key.
The audience - small as it is - starts to chuckle.

> DISSOLVE TO:

INT. COLLINS MUSIC HALL - STAGE WINGS - LATER

Norman[21] is still on stage. The Stage Manager looking
agitated at his pocket watch. Norman[21] is over running.

> DISSOLVE TO:

INT. COLLINS MUSIC HALL - STAGE - CONTINUOUS

Norman[21] still performing shadow boxing and tap dancing,
singing and falling. The small audience lap it up.

> STAGE MANAGER (O.S.)
> Come off!

Norman[21] carries on, and on and the Stage Manager appears
at the wings get's more frustrated.

> STAGE MANAGER (CONT'D)
> Come off now you bloody fool!

Norman[21] ends his act abruptly.

                    NORMAN[21]
          Thank you and Good Night!

                                        DISSOLVE TO:

INT. COLLINS MUSIC HALL - MANAGERS OFFICE

The Hall Manager is counting up the taking in his office. A
TAP on the GLASS DOOR and Norman[21] pops his head around the
door with a cheeky grin.

                    HALL MANAGER
          Oh, Mr Failure, come on in.

Norman[21] enters meekly.

                    HALL MANAGER (CONT'D)
          Well you did it? Congratulations.
          Your first week in show business.

                    NORMAN[21]
          I'm pleased with how it went.

                    HALL MANAGER
          As long as you're happy. The
          audience left you in one piece so
          you can't have been all bad.

                    NORMAN[21]
          No. No.

There is an uneasy silence.

                    NORMAN[21] (CONT'D)
          So, I'll be going now.

                    HALL MANAGER
          OK, well thanks again. Who knows
          one day you might come back to top
          the bill.

                    NORMAN[21]
          Now, that would be great. Anyway, I
          just thought I'd collect my wages
          before I go. If that's OK?

                    HALL MANAGER
          Wages? Oh, yes. Of course.

The hall manager takes £5 from his takings and opens a book
before passing it to Norman[21].

> HALL MANAGER (CONT'D)
> Just sign here, just to say you've
> been paid.

> NORMAN[21]
> Of course.

Norman[21] signs the document.

> HALL MANAGER
> There you go..

And then he pockets the note himself leaving Norman[21]
hanging on to thin air and wondering what has happened.

> HALL MANAGER (CONT'D)
> Commission Norman. Think of it as
> an agent's fee. You'll need to get
> used to that.

Norman[21] is a bit taken back.

> HALL MANAGER (CONT'D)
> Welcome to show business.

Norman[21] composes himself.

> NORMAN[21]
> You know what? Keep it. Like I said
> I'd have paid you for the chance.

> HALL MANAGER
> No need to rub that in.

> NORMAN[21]
> Thanks anyway.

> HALL MANAGER
> Yes, see you around. Oh, hang on.

He retrieves a card from inside his desk and hands it over.

> HALL MANAGER (CONT'D)
> I nearly forgot. This was left at
> the stage door for you. I couldn't
> help reading it.

Norman[21] grips the card.

> HALL MANAGER (CONT'D)
> Seems someone liked you. Some chap
> is putting a show together for
> Portsmouth Coliseum.

Norman[21] speechless.

>   HALL MANAGER (CONT'D)
>   You start Monday so might want to
>   give him a call a bit sharpish.
>   Sorry I should have given it you
>   before, but you know, busy, busy.

>   NORMAN[21]
>   That's unbelievable.

>   HALL MANAGER
>   Yes, isn't it just? Shut the door
>   on the way out. There's a good
>   chap.

>   CUT TO:

INT. COLLINS MUSIC HALL - OUTSIDE MANAGERS OFFICE

Norman[21] slowly closes the door. His face lights up before
he runs down the corridor and jumps to punch the air.

>   CUT TO WHITE:

>   FADE IN:

INT. THEATRE DRESSING ROOM - 1952 - DAY - YEARS LATER

SUPERIMPOSE: "London, 1952."

We transition to slightly older NORMAN[37].

A theatrical poster on the wall now shows Norman Wisdom's
climb to top of the bill is now complete with his
transformation to the "Gump" character with trademark ill
fitting suit and cap.

Norman[37] is preparing for another show in his dressing
room, sitting in front of a stage mirror, when there is a
KNOCK on the DOOR and without delay it opens slightly a jar
and a BILLY MARSH agent pops his head through the gap.

>   BILLY MARSH
>   You decent?

>   NORMAN[37]
>   No but come in anyway.

He does, carrying a large envelope, and closes the door
behind him.

                         BILLY MARSH
          And how is my favorite artiste'?

                         NORMAN[37]
          If you tell me who it is I'll ask
          when I see him.

                         BILLY MARSH
          That's no way to greet an agent
          bearing gifts.

                         NORMAN[37]
          Gifts? That's not the Billy Marsh I
          know and love.

                         BILLY MARSH
          Oh, you're going to love me even
          more dear chap.

Norman[37] is now hooked, wondering what on earth Billy has
come for. He spins round in his chair to face him. Billy
drops the large document sized opened envelope, that THUDS
down on the work area in front of Norman[37]. Leaving
Norman[37] even more intrigued.

                         NORMAN[37]
          What..?

Billy puts his hands on the arms of Norman[37]'s chair and
spins him round so they are face to face. He leans in.

                         BILLY MARSH
          One word.

He pauses for effect, Norman[37] is hanging.

                         BILLY MARSH (CONT'D)
          Rank!

A second to decode, then.

                         NORMAN[37]
          You're kidding?

                         BILLY MARSH
          I never joke about money.

                         NORMAN[37]
          When? What? Tell me!

                         BILLY MARSH
          Mr J Arthur Rank, wishes to sign
          you, the artist, Norman Wisdom, on
          an exclusive seven year deal at..

Norman[37] can hardly believe what he is hearing.

                    BILLY MARSH (CONT'D)
          ..Five thousand per movie!

                    NORMAN[37]
          Billy!

Billy stands back and Norman[37] is out of his seat and they
give each other a celebratory hug before they can calm down
enough to talk.

                    NORMAN[37] (CONT'D)
          When?, I mean what happens now?

                    BILLY MARSH
          You sign, we celebrate! No screen
          test, no small print, no opt outs.
          This is unheard of my boy. They
          want you and they're willing to pay
          through the nose for you. And it
          will be my pleasure to make sure
          they do.

Norman[37] drops back in his seat.

                    NORMAN[37]
          Pinch me Billy.

                    BILLY MARSH
          I'd rather kiss you! This is the
          big time Norman. You're going to be
          the biggest home grown movie comic
          this country has ever seen.

Norman[37] tilts his head back and closes his eyes.

                                                  CUT TO:

EXT. BUCKINGHAMSHIRE PINEWOOD - DAY - SOME WEEKS LATER

A Bentley car weaves it way through the countryside.

                                                  CUT TO:

INT. BENTLEY CAR - CONTINUOUS

As Norman[37] opens his eyes. Billy sits in the back with him
as his chauffeur drives them towards Pinewood studio's
impressive entrance.

                         NORMAN[37]
              What happened to no screen tests?

                         BILLY MARSH
              Let them call it whatever they
              want. The ink on the contract is
              dry. They're into you for five
              movies in the next seven years,
              come what may. Today is all about
              meeting the director and reading
              through their script. That's all.

Norman[37] doesn't look too convinced.

                    BILLY MARSH (CONT'D)
                       (reassuring)
              A formality. Relax!

                                             CUT TO:

INT. PINEWOOD STUDIOS - LATER

Typical movie studios, big lights and film cameras. Movie
crew milling. The Set has been dressed to represent an
intimate candle lit dinner for two. The Director RONALD NEAME
is setting up the shots in the background and talking to
PETULA CLARKE. In the foreground Norman[37] is getting more
nervous as he chats with Billy before the Director's
attention turns to him.

                         NORMAN[37]
                       (whisper)
              Petula Clarke?

                         BILLY MARSH
              Only the best for you. You lucky
              little devil. This Neame chap, has
              just shot a film with Gregory Peck
              about a Million Pound Note of all
              things, so they're not messing
              about Norm.

                         NORMAN[37]
              That's just it. I want to mess
              about. That's what I do best. Have
              you read this script?

                         BILLY MARSH
              No, I'm not in the picture you are.
              Why would I be reading the script?

Norman[37] tilts his hand to read the script.

                         NORMAN[37]
          "Norman stares into Petula's eyes
          and takes her hand..."

                         BILLY MARSH
               Really?

He snatches the script off Norman[37] to look at.

                         BILLY MARSH (CONT'D)
          Oh, look there's a kiss too. You
          really are a lucky little devil.

                         NORMAN[37]
          Billy. This isn't me!

                         BILLY MARSH
          Five thousand a movie and you get
          to kiss Petula Clarke. I wish it
          was me.

An ASSISTANT approaches Norman[37] to break the news.

                         ASSISTANT
          Excuse me, Mr Wisdom? If we could
          have you on set now Mr Neame would
          like to walk through the script
          with you.

                                        CUT TO:

INT. PINEWOOD STUDIOS - LATER

Norman[37] and Petula are seated opposite in their romantic
scene. Looking deep into each others eyes.

                         NORMAN[37]
                 (romantic)
          Your eyes are as light as gossamer.

                         RONALD NEAME
               Cut.

Norman[37] and Petula snap out of their characters and each
sit back.

                         RONALD NEAME (CONT'D)
          Petula you're wonderful. Norman,
          I'm not feeling it. Let's try that
          again from the top?

                         NORMAN[37]
          It's these lines?

                    RONALD NEAME
               (touchy)
          What's wrong with the lines?

                    NORMAN[37]
          Eyes light as gossamer? How is that
          even possible?

Petula puts her hand to her mouth to suppress a giggle. Billy
is cringing from behind the camera and gesturing to
Norman[37] to keep quiet.

                    RONALD NEAME
          From the top please. Roll cameras.

A CLAPPER BOARD fills the screen and SLAMS shut in front of
the pair.

                    RONALD NEAME (O.S.) (CONT'D)
          Action!

                                        CUT TO:

INT. BENTLEY CAR - LATER

The mood is bleak. Norman[37] and Billy Marsh in stoney
silence. Norman[37] rests his arm on the door arm rest and
sits with his hand over his mouth.

                                        DISSOLVE TO:

INT. BILLY MARSH'S OFFICE - SOME WEEKS LATER

Billy finishes looking at a letter and drops it on his desk.

                    BILLY MARSH
          I can't sugar coat it. They want
          out Norm?

Norman[37] shakes his head.

                    BILLY MARSH (CONT'D)
          They've pulled the plug on the
          picture but they will pay in full.
          Not a bad amount for one kiss.

                    NORMAN[37]
          What about the other films? I've
          got a seven year exclusive
          contract. Remember? "Come what
          may." I think you said.

                    BILLY MARSH
          They're going back to the drawing
          board. Rethinking the roles they
          have in mind. It's not good.

                    NORMAN[37]
          There will be other films though?
          You are sure about that?

His head sways a little. He holds up the letter.

                    BILLY MARSH
          Reading this, it wouldn't surprise
          me if they tried to buy you out of
          the contract altogether. It won't
          be anything like five thousand a
          movie but it'll be the easiest
          money you've ever made.

                    NORMAN[37]
          No Billy. Even if they offer the
          full amount it's a no. We've got a
          contract to make movies. If I
          hadn't signed with them I could
          have signed with ABC. I bet I
          wouldn't have this problem now
          either. It's the writers at Rank
          who are to blame, not me. They're
          still in the twenties.

                    BILLY MARSH
          That contract is solid so I'll
          throw that back at them. We can't
          force them to make the movies but
          if they know we won't accept a
          penny less than contracted they
          might not pull the plug completely.

                    NORMAN[37]
          New writers. Tell them we need new
          writers. Someone who understands
          the ordinary working man. Otherwise
          it just won't work.

Billy holds up his hands to say he'll do it.

                                        CUT TO:

EXT. HAMPSHIRE GARDEN - DAY - SOME WEEKS LATER

The sun is shining and a comfortable looking couple are
sitting on their patio enjoying the weather.

MICHAEL FOOT and JILL CRAIGIE sit opposite each other, both facing a typewriter and each typing away independently.

SUPERIMPOSE: "Michael Foot, Politician."

                MICHAEL FOOT
    Dear, what you think of this?

He sits up a little to deliver. His wife, JILL CRAIGIE, stops what she is doing to offer her full attention. He milks it for all it's worth.

                MICHAEL FOOT (CONT'D)
        (shakespearean)
    In view of the fact that many of
    the recommendations contained in
    this Select Committee's Report
    merely repeat recommendations made
    by the Committee as long ago as
    1927 does not the right hon.
    Gentleman think that there should
    be the most earnest consideration
    given to these recommendations?

                JILL CRAIGIE
    Oh, very good dear.

                MICHAEL FOOT
    Thank you. Do you think they'll
    take any notice?

                JILL CRAIGIE
    I have no idea darling. But at
    least they'll know you mean
    business and you're not to be
    trifled with.

                MICHAEL FOOT
        (pleased)
    Emm, yes indeed.

She goes back to her work but he still wants to talk.

                MICHAEL FOOT (CONT'D)
        (tentative)
    What are you working on dear?

SUPERIMPOSE: "Jill Craigie, Screenwriter."

                JILL CRAIGIE
    I'm writing a piece for the working
    man too. But I'm hoping mine might
    get a few more laughs.

                    MICHAEL FOOT
        Oh.

They both start typing again, on the table is a draft of a
screenplay the title, "Trouble in Store".

                                    DISSOLVE TO:

INT. PINEWOOD STUDIOS - 1953 - DAY

SUPERIMPOSE: PINEWOOD STUDIOS 1953 "Trouble in Store"

Typical busy London street scene. A Policeman stops the flow
of traffic and an open topped chauffeur driven Rolls Royce
car can be seen waiting for the flow to restart. In the back
seat a high flying business man and, it appears, next to him
Norman[37] as "Norman Pitkin."

The Policeman starts the traffic flow again and the car moves
forward showing Norman Pitkin is actually sitting on a
bicycle alongside the car.

Norman Pitkin catches up with the car and comes to the
foreground. As the car stops again he rests his hand on the
side of the car. The business man tries to flick his hand off
with a glove but Norman Pitkin is too quick and moves his
hand back and forth so he keeps missing until the car pulls
forward again causing Norman Pitkin to fall from his bike.

                    VOICE (O.S.)
        Cut and Print!

The back projected street scene disappears, there is CLAPPING
and CHEERS and LAUGHING all around. Assistants rush on and
take the bike from Norman[37]. Everyone seems pleased.

                                    END FLASHBACK.

                                    FADE IN:

INT. BAFTA AWARDS - 1954 - BACK TO PRESENT DAY

SUPERIMPOSE: "BAFTA AWARDS NIGHT - 1954."

The COMPERE at the lectern..

                    COMPERE
        ..'Most Promising Newcomer to
        Film..' (beat) And the winner is..

The sound FADES AWAY with images IN SLOW MOTION dreamlike
state as everyone around Norman[37] starts to clap in silence
and look and smile at him.

He rises from the table with a great smile on his face and
starts to make his way to the stage..

                                            FADE TO BLACK.

                                            FADE IN:

EXT. KENT COAST ROAD - DAY

Gradually the sound of a MOTORBIKE ROAR can be heard in the
distance, getting nearer.

The road signs point the way to Kent. The coast road
stretches out in front of us as a MOTORBIKE ROARS in to shot.

                                            CUT TO:

EXT. KENT COAST ROAD - LATER

The Motorbike slows to a stop. In the background, a coal
merchants and workers busy loading coal on wagons.

The rider dismounts, removes his helmet and we can see
Norman[37] who walks towards the workers. One of them looks
at the approaching man. A few beats of strained recognition.
The worker is an older Fred.

Fred stands straight and drops his shovel slowly walking
towards Norman. Then once both men are sure, the last few
paces are taken quickly and they embrace each other.

                                            FADE OUT.

Printed in Great Britain
by Amazon